Unity:
a Quest for Truth

Eric Butterworth

Unity Books
Unity Village, MO 64065

Unity: a Quest for Truth was originally
published by Robert Speller & Sons,
Publishers, Inc.

Fifteen printings through 1984.

Second edition, Unity Books
Second printing, 1988

Second edition © 1985 by Unity School of Christianity
Unity Village, MO 64065
Library of Congress Card No. 85-050997
ISBN 0-87159-165-0

Unity:
a Quest for Truth

Table of Contents

Introduction

Introduction

Psychologists have estimated that not one person in a million is living up to the best that is in him or her. Are you? Are you making the most of your inner resources?

When you ride a bus or walk down the street, look into the faces of others and try to imagine what life would be like if all these people should suddenly awaken and become their best possible selves. But, before you become too smug, take a look in a mirror and ask what your life would be like if you released your "imprisoned splendor."

The wisdom of the ages is not limited to the

tomes of the past. Most of it still lies locked in the depths of our mental potential. The capacity for health and eternal life lies undeveloped within our life potential. The key to the kingdom of all-sufficiency with work and food and abundance for all humankind still lies unused in the depths of our undiscovered faculty of faith.

In the past hundred years the world has seen its frontiers disappear. Today the last remaining frontier is in the realm of Spirit. In the face of the awesome challenges confronting us, there is nowhere to go but *in.* The next great step of humankind is the "adventure into God."

Everywhere people are reexamining the world's religions, looking for guideposts for the new spiritual adventure. However, as historian Arnold Toynbee says: *One of the greatest challenges facing mankind today is the challenge to traditional religion to find a present-day faith that corresponds with present-day needs.*

In this book we want to introduce to you a movement that has faced this challenge and is evolving an open-ended stream of helpful concepts that fill this need. We will briefly consider the background of the Unity movement and how it has come out of the world religious stream. We will also touch lightly upon some of the basic Unity concepts.

The challenge to religion today is to recognize and teach that:

God is not only the God of history . . . He is also the God of today.

The supreme Power of the universe is not locked in ancient Scriptures but is alive in the world now.

Revelation is not a special dispensation of God but a quality of Divine Mind and a faculty of our minds.

What God is revealing to us today may be more important than what He said to us yesterday.

All of us have a right to expect our religion to help us find spiritual unity with God, to find the same source of inspiration within as did the prophets of old, to find the same healing power that was demonstrated by Jesus, and to: *Let this mind be in you, which was also in Christ Jesus.* (Phil. 2:5, A.V.)

Unity has been devoted to helping people to realize this spiritual unity with God for nearly 100 years. It works through prayer but with a new science of prayer. It works in the field of spiritual healing, but with a new technique of spiritual healing. It works for prosperity, but with a new definition of prosperity, a new awareness of God's will for abundance. It works for peace among all people, but it is a: . . . *Peace . . . which passes all understanding . . . .* (Phil. 4:7)

Unity has been in the forefront of the new religious concern for self-management of the mind. Unity says that the mind is the connecting link between God and humanity. Unity has been a silent catalyst in many fields of search and research—giving rise to the popular technique of positive thinking, inspiring the laboratory quest for the extra-sensory link between the finite and the infinite in all people. It may also have contributed much of the incentive as well as the basic premises in the search for emotional causes of illness in the field of psychosomatic medicine.

Unity is an ecumenical movement. It is not a program for uniting religious organizations into one ecclesiastical body, but a teaching movement seeking to lead all people—regardless of organizational barriers or theological differences—to a new sense of spiritual unity with God and with one another.

Unity is not a church but an institution for scientific self-discovery and self-unfoldment. It asks not, "What is your background, your religious affiliation, your state or station in life?" It asks only, "What is your interest, your aspiration, your vision of life?" Unity students are a strange and wonderful fellowship of people of all religious affiliations, of all races, of all levels of the social structure, meeting on the level of their spiritual unity with each other in the common quest for spiritual unity with God.

World headquarters of the Unity movement is at Unity Village, Missouri, just southeast of Kansas City. Unity School of Christianity publishes millions of pieces of printed matter each year. Best known is the daily devotional magazine, DAILY WORD. WEE WISDOM is the oldest children's magazine in the United States in continuous publication. UNITY Magazine contains articles on metaphysics and positive living. And there are now about 450 local affiliated Unity centers throughout the world—in most states of the U.S., and in Great Britain, West Germany, Nigeria, Australia, the West Indies, Venezuela, Colombia, and New Zealand. There are study groups in such countries as

Austria, Switzerland, Holland, Ecuador, Mexico, India, and the Virgin Islands.

If this book whets your appetite to know more about Unity, the next step is up to you. There may be a Unity center in your community. Consult the telephone directory, or write Unity School of Christianity, Unity Village, Missouri 64065. They will send you introductory material that will acquaint you with the scope of the movement, its literature, its prayer activities, the educational programs, and the fellowship retreats.

So after this brief introduction, and with the intent to answer in greater depth, let us ask the question, "What is Unity?"

Eric Butterworth

1

The Relentless Stream
of Truth

A planeload of clergymen were returning from a religious convocation in Honolulu. Just past the point of no return one of the engines died. A stewardess dutifully walked the aisle giving assurances that everything would be all right.

Thinking that the young lady needed some reassurance herself, one of the ministers said, "Young lady, there is nothing to worry about. You see, there are eight bishops on board." The stewardess replied, "Thank you, sir, I'll convey that message to the captain."

Soon she was back. The minister said, "I

see you told the captain. What did he say?"
The girl tartly replied, "He said he would
rather have four good engines."

There are millions of people in the world
today who have either given up on or have
never believed in religion. These people say,
in effect, "I would rather have a good job,
money in the bank, a healthy body, a circle of
loved ones, a world at peace, than the promise
of a reward in some vague afterlife." In ages
past, such talk would have been rank heresy.
Today it is so common a reaction that it
hardly raises an eyebrow.

With the marvelous innovations of modern
science, it might appear to many that, because we have engines for our cars and boats,
motors for our elevators and dishwashers,
and jet engines for our airplanes, we have
little need for bishops or other spiritual
leaders. For illness we turn to the doctor, for
guidance we turn to the psychologist, for our
daily bread we turn to the marketplace. It
might be said that for many, even though
they turn regularly to their church on Sunday
morning, it is more for prestige or by habit
than for any real search for Truth.

But the churchgoing habit is a good habit.
More people would do well to cultivate it.

However, it is doubtful that there will be any great resurgence of interest in churchgoing, other than for purposes of "conventional respectability," until there is a renaissance of the practical, demonstrable, and scientific in their ethic.

A religion, to be a contemporary influence, must be redefined for every generation in the light of that day's thought. Few religions in all history have done this. Thus religion invariably has taken recourse in symbols, in ritual, form, dogma, and a worship experience that eventually becomes little more than mechanical.

And yet we are incurably religious. There is an inner restlessness in us that is never fully satisfied until we find God. As it was said by Michel Eyquem de Montaigne: *We are born to inquire after Truth.* In our day the quest for Truth is normally pursued (even by many who are formally religious) in modern psychology, philosophy, existentialism, or Zen Buddhism, in political idealogies, and in mystic works of poetry. For many, it leads into the field of metaphysics and what is called New Thought. Perhaps it has led you to this book.

If Unity were a sect within Christianity,

with established creeds and traditional forms of worship, it would be a relatively simple matter to answer the question, "What is Unity?" For reasons that will become obvious as these lessons unfold, this is not the case, and the question has no simple answer. We are going to outline something of the background, the ideals, the objectives of Unity; but in the final analysis the question, "What is Unity?" will be answered by you in terms of what Unity means to you.

It is not easy to mark one date as the beginning of Unity. It started as a movement in the minds of Charles and Myrtle Fillmore, two earnest searchers for Truth whose lives were spent in a relentless quest through religions and philosophies of the world. If we must settle on one particular movement as the starting point of what we today think of as the Unity movement, we might say it was in Kansas City in the spring of 1886.

Charles and Myrtle Fillmore, facing physical and financial crises that seemed insurmountable, attended a lecture by Dr. E. B. Weeks, who was a representative of the Illinois Metaphysical College, then headed by Emma Curtis Hopkins. Something strange happened to Myrtle Fillmore at this time. It was no mystical experience or emotional conversion. It was simply that as she left the lecture, a new, different, liberating, transforming conviction was blazing in her heart and mind. She had been raised under the belief of hereditary weakness, and was at that time living under medical sentence of "a few months to live" due to a tubercular condition. She walked out of the meeting repeating over and over in her mind: *I am a child of God and therefore I do not inherit sickness.*

Unity as a movement began at that moment, for it led to complete healing for Myrtle Fillmore (who lived forty years beyond that time), and the healing of Charles Fillmore of physical and financial trouble. It led to study and research of Truth that resulted in some amazing discoveries and some wonderful demonstrations of help and healing.

With a selflessness that has always been a common characteristic of inspired people, the Fillmores gave much time to helping and teaching their friends and neighbors. At first there was no attempt to organize in a formal way. They simply helped those who asked. And, as the word of their great work spread, there were many who asked. Almost before they knew it, and without any desire to do so on their part, they found themselves in a new lifework of helping others find this understanding of Truth.

Unity did not originate as an offshoot of any Christian sect or denomination. It was in the beginning, and remains today, a banding together of students seeking Truth. There was no effort in the beginning, and through the years there has been none, to organize local centers or churches by missionary work. This phase of Unity has simply evolved.

The little prayer group composed of the Fillmores and their close friends were originally called "The Society of Silent Help." In the beginning this group was the whole of Unity. Today, even though Unity encircles the globe with its periodicals numbering into the millions of copies each month, and regardless of the fact that Unity centers and churches may be found in nearly every city of fair size in the United States and Canada, this prayer group, now known as Silent Unity, is still the heart of the Unity work. Through the years, millions of prayer requests have been received and personally answered by this unique prayer organization and thousands of positive (often called "miracles") results have been achieved in the lives of people all over the world. Silent Unity has approximately two hundred workers.

In 1888 Charles Fillmore started a little magazine called "Modern Thought," which is the forerunner of today's UNITY Magazine. It was a literary forum devoted to discussion and exchange of ideas by and for people on the quest for Truth. At one time this periodical was called "Christian Science Thought." This has caused many to believe that Unity was once associated with and is an offshoot of Christian Science. In that day the term *Christian science* was a term as universal as the word *Truth* is today. It referred not to an organization but to a general approach to Christianity. Eventually, Mary Baker Eddy, head of the Christian Science Church, won the exclusive legal right to the term, so Unity discontinued using it. As you will read later, there is a striking and quite understandable similarity between the teachings of Unity and Christian Science, but no direct relationship.

We might wonder why such a movement as Unity came into being. We know it was formulated by the Fillmores, but why was Myrtle Fillmore unable to find satisfaction in her membership in the Methodist Church,

and why did Charles Fillmore find all
churches unpalatable to his thinking mind?
Some years ago there appeared an article in
The Atlantic Monthly written by a promi-
nent Englishman. He called attention to the
fact that there was a profound desire for religion in the world that no church or sect
seemed to be satisfying. He closed his article
with these significant words:

*The question remains, which no one yet can
answer, whether any existing church has the
energy to grasp the full-orbed conception of
the Kingdom of Heaven, both as an inner and
an outer thing, to free itself from its own past,
to proclaim the truth that Christianity is yet
to be discovered by all the powers of man's
mind, and to be practiced by all the energy of
his will. If not, we may dare to predict that a
new Church will arise and destroy the old
ones.*

Unity in no way claims to be the "new
church" herein mentioned, for it does not
consider itself to be a church in a real sense.
Nor does it agree that "the old ones" must
be destroyed. It is obvious, however, that
movements such as Unity have come into
being as a direct result of the failure of
traditional Christian churches to realize that

"Christianity is yet to be discovered." Unity is dedicated simply to helping people both within and without the Christian churches to make that discovery for themselves. While some people claim a Unity center as their church home, many who are helped and influenced by the Unity teachings consider Unity a supplementary faith and continue as members in good standing in their own churches.

Every religion of the world had its beginning in the inspiration and revelation of an individual. All sacred writings (certainly including our Bible), all creeds and rituals, all institutions of every religion in the world are the product, not the cause, of these firsthand experiences in the inner lives of various people. The people who have made religion a vital power for any age are those who believed they stood face to face with God, and heard His voice or felt His presence in their souls. Thus, the sacred writings of all religious faiths were not miraculously prepared and let down from the skies, but were simply the written experiences of people in all ages who felt they had a special revelation of truth they wanted to convey to others.

All the religions of the world reveal a common pattern of evolution. They began in a moment of inspiration in one great life. Then followed a period of teaching and healing. This was usually followed by a similar period of teaching and healing by students and disciples. After this there was usually an organization of a movement to perpetuate the ideas and memory of the founder. And finally the organization is devoted almost exclusively to the worship of the founder.

Christianity is no exception, but is, in fact, a good case in point. Somewhere after the age of the disciples and the widespread ministry of Paul, there developed a strong machine-like organization that created creeds and doctrines by majority vote of bishops or cardinals. Once created, these creeds and doctrines became inviolable, whether or not they had any similarity with Jesus' teachings. In time the "machine" of the Christian church was synchronized with the machinations of the Roman Empire, which then became "Holy." Conversion to Christianity was enforced by punishment of resistance. Anti-Christians were put to death. During the Inquisition alone some 32,000 people were burned at the stake "in the name of Jesus," for little more than daring to think.

Eventually the Protestant Reformation

came as a revolt from the authority of the Roman Church. It began as a sincere demand that the individual had the right to worship God as he or she chose. Soon the Protestant leaders and the movements they organized were also unwilling for anyone to object to them, and the hangings and burnings at the stake continued, only under a different regime.

The problem that any religious movement has always faced is the desire of the individual to have a personal experience with God. This desire of men and women has always been completely incompatible with the ideas of the religious "machines" which have perpetuated the idea that relationship with God must come through the organization or its priests or clergy. Ralph Waldo Emerson asked the question in his famous Divinity School Address in 1838: Why should *we* not have a firsthand and immediate experience of God? Thinking people through the ages have asked the same question.

One characteristic found in all churches is the devotion to the preservation and promulgation of "ancient doctrines" and "historic creeds." They make every effort to protect the existing order and to maintain things as they are. But unfortunately, while institutions, systems, beliefs, and even ideals tend to become static, people have forever been dynamic beings. In the nature of things, humankind can never be satisfied with "things as they are." In just the measure that we become content, we cease to aspire and thus, cease to fully live. Thinking people have always instinctively known that true religion is bigger than its organizations, better than its adherents, and more vital than its creeds and rituals.

It was perfectly normal for people like Charles and Myrtle Fillmore to ask, as did Emerson, "Why can *we* not have a firsthand experience of God?" Charles Fillmore, after finding so many conflicting statements about God, wrote in an early publication of "Modern Thought": *In this Babel, I will go to "headquarters." God and I can somehow communicate, or the whole thing is a fraud.*

Because Unity is not an offshoot of any Christian church organization, its teachings have not been formulated by revising or adapting historic creeds. Unity looks backward beyond the time of church organization to the teachings and the ministry of Jesus Christ as they transpired. The Unity teachings today are directed, even as Jesus' teachings were directed, toward a "firsthand experience of God."

Charles Fillmore has been the guiding light through the years in the quest for a practical and workable Christianity. But Unity is by no means limited to the writings of Charles Fillmore, nor is it a formula definition of the Truth of God and man. Truth cannot be put into a formula.

Charles Fillmore disliked dogma. However, eventually students induced him to write out a statement of faith. It could easily have been the turning point of the movement into a fixed and final teaching, the pollution and stagnation of the flow of the relentless stream of Truth. Making a set statement of faith would be the most serious crisis Unity could ever meet. Charles Fillmore was equal to the challenge, however, for he qualified his "Statement of Faith" with the words: *We have considered the restrictions that will follow a formulated platform, and are hereby giving warning that we shall not be bound by this tentative statement of what Unity believes. We may change our minds tomorrow on some of the points, and if we do, we shall feel free to make a new statement. . . .* Thus the points of Unity's "Statement of Faith" have never become the basic creed of the Unity movement. Today it is seldom used. This point alone might go a long way toward answering the question, "What is Unity?"

Unity is often referred to as a "return to first-century Christianity," "primitive Christianity," or "practical Christianity." The word *practical* is a relative term. Anything may be practical when people are ready to regard it as such and put it to the test. Anything may be impractical so long as people are unwilling to test it out in actual experience. Thus, the term "practical Christianity" is not intended to imply that Unity is a religion that is essentially different from that subscribed to by orthodox Christianity. It is not that Unity is practical while some other Christian discipline is impractical. Unity is called "practical Christianity" simply because the Unity ideal is the actual *practice* of Jesus' teachings on a seven-day-a-week basis.

Christianity, wherever it is taught, when shorn of its superficial ritual and dogma, can become amazingly practical as a therapy for all human ills. One of the great roles that Unity has played through the years is in the influence it has among hundreds of thousands of Christians (of many denominations) toward better understanding and demonstration of the workable principles hidden within their own religion.

Essentially, Unity is not a new religion. It is not a new philosophy or a new teaching. Unity is purely and simply a technique in the demonstration and practice of Christian principles—principles that have been understood and practiced by the few through all ages. A good example of a practical concept of Christianity that seems to reflect but actually predates by many centuries the Unity viewpoint, is the philosophy of Brother Lawrence, a lay priest of the Middle Ages. His philosophy is outlined in the dynamic little book, "The Practice of the Presence of God." (Not available from Unity School of Christianity.)

To rightly understand and appreciate Christianity, we must realize that what Jesus taught and practiced was not a new set of spiritual principles. He said: *"Think not that I have come to abolish the law and the prophets; I have come not to abolish them but to fulfill them."* (Matt. 5:17) Jesus accomplished His great works and attained to the level of Christhood because of His consciousness of the ageless and universal Truth. We like to think of Jesus as the Supreme Revealer of the Truth to all people. But His teaching, which we call Christianity, is universal Truth presented in the form of dynamic techniques for understanding and demonstrating from the power of our oneness with God.

Accept this point and you begin to see that all through the ages there have been those who have clearly or dimly perceived Truth. The relentless stream of Truth has known no boundaries. It has flowed through the minds and hearts of both churchgoers and the unchurched alike. We can find evidence of the stream of Truth in the thinking of Plato, Socrates, Aristotle, and other Greek philosophers. We find it in St. Augustine, St. Francis, Thomas Aquinas, Meister Eckehart, and other religious leaders. We find it in Galileo, Copernicus, Newton, Einstein, and others in the field of science. We find it in Hegel, Kant, Schopenhauer, and other philosophers. And we find it singing through the words of poets and essayists like Shakespeare, Browning, Tennyson, Carlyle, and Emerson.

Many who have moved by or within the relentless stream of Truth have been branded atheists and agnostics, simply because their concepts dared to differ from the musty creeds that prevailed in their day. If it was their misfortune to live during certain "dark periods" of history, they may have been persecuted and even burned at the stake for their differences.

In America during the seventeenth century you would have been liable to burning at the stake for considering such things as you are right now, looking at religion with an open mind, insisting upon a "firsthand experience with God."

Anne Hutchinson was a devout worshiper in the congregation of Joseph Cotton in Boston. She organized a group to meet in her home to study and discuss his teachings. They formed a prayer group for personal development and what today we might call group therapy. There was no precedent for such a thing in Puritan Christianity. The result was a series of harassing persecutions that eventually concluded in the hanging of several of her associates, and somewhat later, she was, as it has been written: *hung up as a flag for others to take example from.* Anne Hutchinson, seeking only to apply Christianity in everyday experience, was hung on Boston Common by those who, having fought for the right to worship God according to their own fashion, were unwilling that any should worship God otherwise.

Praise God that we have progressed much since that day. Anne Hutchinson might well have been a forerunner of the Unity ideal, for Unity today is dedicated to the open mind, to the continuous quest for Truth. It seeks not to tell you *what* to think, how to define God, what creeds to accept. Unity seeks only to teach you *how* to think, how to pray—so that you can formulate your own definition of God, experience your own communion with God, and find your own distinctly personal revelation of Truth.

What is the difference between Unity and other similar organizations in the New Thought movement? Most have a common origin, not in a common schism in Christianity, but in a common flow of the relentless stream of Truth. At the turn of the nineteenth century, amid the Industrial Revolution (which brought social and economic changes all over the world) there was a corresponding spiritual awakening felt by many thinking people. Tennyson, in his later years, once remarked to a friend: *My chief desire is to have a new vision of God.* It was a spontaneous and universal hunger for Truth.

Unlike the Protestant Reformation, this awakening was no schism within the Church. Nor was it truly a defection from it. It was essentially a movement of idealism, religious liberalism, and a sincere search for the practical Truth that frees. The term *New Thought* never did designate a specific movement or organization. Emerson used the words in referring to "this new thought." W. John Murray popularized the term at the turn of the twentieth century in his phrase: "The New Thought of Man, the Larger Thought of God."

The one man who unwittingly played the major role in America in the formulation of the ideas we now refer to as New Thought was Phineas Parker Quimby (1802-1868) in New England. He conducted many experiments in mental and spiritual healing, and had a large following of students. Among many who studied with Quimby was a woman by the name of Mary Baker Patterson (later to be known as Mary Baker Eddy). Much of the idealism that she later formulated into Christian Science was influenced by Quimby. She was but one of many who went on to teach and spread the so-called New Thought doctrine.

We have already pointed to the influence on the Fillmores and the development of Unity of a New Thought lecturer named E. B. Weeks. It is likely that Nona Brooks, the founder of Divine Science, and Ernest Holmes, founder of Religious Science, and others, had a similar beginning. All apparently came out of a common stream of idealism. These ideals have been developed in various ways, with emphasis placed in many differing areas of Truth.

Perhaps the one distinction between the many organizations within the Truth movement of today and Unity is that Unity has centered its attention on interpreting and articulating the teachings of Jesus Christ. Unity considers itself wholly Christian, with Jesus Christ as its true authority.

Charles Fillmore wrote: *Christ Truth, it seems to me, is of vastly greater importance than any amount of theorizing about the existence of heaven or hell, or life after death, or how we should be sprinkled or plunged in order to be saved. To one who gains even a meager quickening of the Spirit, Christianity ceases to be a theory; it becomes a demonstrable science of the mind.*

What is the object and goal of Unity?

Unity is not seeking to have Unity centers or churches on every corner. Unity desires to be not a powerful organization, but a powerful influence for good in individual lives. It seeks not to be *the* religion, but to help people find religion for and within themselves.

There are many definitions of religion, but it is Unity's belief that the essence of religion is the consciousness of God. The ultimate goal of the teaching of Unity is to help you to become one with God, not just to become bound through membership or other obligation to an organization. This is another sense in which Unity does not consider itself a church. The church has always tended to lay stress on sacraments, creeds, baptism, manner of worship, etc.

The interesting thing is that the really great spiritual thinkers of every age, both within and without the organized church, have clearly recognized that the only salvation worthy of the name is the life that results from spiritual unity with God.

This is what religion meant to Jesus. He felt Himself to be one with God. To Him God was not a formula to be explained, or a dogma to be believed, least of all a name to conjure by. God was the wondrous life welling up in

Him, the true essence of His Selfhood. This was to Jesus an actual experience in consciousness, but He knew it was an experience possible to all men and women, once they would awaken to the meaning of their own Selfhood.

As its name implies, Unity has been a unifying influence in all spiritual seeking. However, Unity would never favor a unity of sameness or uniformity such as is the goal of the ecumenical movement, seeking to unite the whole Christian Church into one body. As long as people differ in temperament, they will prefer and choose different forms of worship. As long as they differ in mind, in education, in experience, they will approach Truth from different viewpoints and interpret their experiences of Truth in different terms. It would mean a tragic loss to religion, to Truth, to life itself, if it should ever be possible to force all people to feel and think and act alike in matters of religion.

Thus, Unity also avoids a unity of sameness within organized religion. It seeks only to present techniques through which people of all backgrounds and beliefs might better practice or demonstrate spiritual law.

There is nothing so peculiarly one's own as

one's religion, because nothing proceeds so directly from that person's deepest, most divine Self. He may express it in different ways and use different symbols and means of devotion, but there is always something deeper than this, the spiritual consciousness that wells up in his being.

The only authoritative creed is the creed people make for themselves, and that creed should be kept constantly open to revision with the coming of every fresh ray of light; the only compelling form of worship will be that to which a person's whole being responds instinctively and spontaneously; and the only church to which he or she will give allegiance will be the church to whose spiritual life and message he is irresistibly drawn.

Emerson once wrote that *a sect or party is an elegant incognito devised to save a man from the vexation of thinking.* Unity is no sect in this sense. There will be no attempt to keep you from thinking. As a matter of fact, unless you are willing to think about Truth, to think through your relationship with God, to think as you pray and to pray as you think, there is little that Unity can offer you.

The lofty ideal of Unity as an open-ended religion for today seems to have been clearly

stated by Robert Browning in his poem
"Paracelsus," which says in part:

> *Truth is within ourselves; it takes no rise*
> *From outward things, whate'er you may*
> *   believe.*
> *There is an inmost centre in us all,*
> *Where truth abides in fullness; and*
> *   around,*
> *Wall upon wall, the gross flesh hems it in,*
> *This perfect, clear perception—which is*
> *   truth.*
> *A baffling and perverting carnal mesh*
> *Binds it, and makes all error: and, to*
> *   KNOW,*
> *Rather consists in opening out a way*
> *Whence the imprisoned splendour may*
> *   escape,*
> *Than in effecting entry for a light*
> *Supposed to be without.*

2

Emphasis On You

It might seem perfectly natural, in a short outline of a teaching such as this, to launch right into the "credo" of beliefs, the concepts and definitions that distinguish Unity from other Christian philosophies. We could give a series of definitions, such as:

God is Spirit, Infinite Mind, the principle of absolute good expressed in all creation.

We are an idea in Divine Mind, the apex of God's creation, created in God's image and likeness.

Christ is the perfect idea of God for us.

Jesus is the perfect expression of the divine idea human form.

Jesus Christ is a union of the two, the idea and the expression—perfect humanity demonstrated.

We could go on down the list giving definitions. However, though they are perfectly good and comprehensive definitions, in an introductory lesson it is important to recognize that to define a thing is to limit it.

We live in a world of words; terms and letters often restrict rather than articulate meanings, and become the agencies of endless misunderstanding. You do not become a mathematician by memorizing all the answers at the back of the book, nor do you become spiritual by memorizing a lot of definitions or building a vocabulary of metaphysical terminology.

A schoolboy, pointing to a tree, asked the teacher, "What is this?" The teacher confidently replied, "That is a tree." He might have added, "We know it is a tree, for we named it ourselves." But the question remains unanswered, "What is a tree?" What is the mystery of that intangible something which expands from a tiny seed and surrounds itself with bark?

Unity is not a creed to accept or an abundance of definitions to memorize. Unity essentially is a technique through which you can find answers for yourself in words that are meaningful to you.

In this chapter we will think about God, about Jesus Christ, and about the Bible. However, we will not consider them as facets of a religion that can be professed separate from life and living, but as keys to our own self-discovery. In every case the emphasis will be on you.

There was once a belief that religion began with a full knowledge of one true God and that thereafter through human fault and disobedience the light of that first splendid vision was clouded or lost. But this is not the story of the assembled records. The story of religion is not a recessional. The worship of sticks and stones is not religion fallen into the dark; it is religion rising out of the dark. The primitive superstitions and the early religions are religious awakening of humanity and the first suppliant gesture toward the unseen.

Why did humankind make the gesture? Because "we are incurably religious." We are innately spiritual beings and have an insatiable hunger for Truth through which our hearts are ever restless until they find repose in the knowledge of God. But regardless of where or what the religious expressions might have been all through the ages, the confidence that there is a power or powers to help has lit the fires on every altar, built every temple, made every creed articulate, and supported every prayer.

Through the ages it is obvious that concepts of God have changed and evolved. Much of our confusion in the study of the Bible comes from the fact that the God of the Israelites was a stern, autocratic, and sometimes cruel God, a God of vengeance who destroyed whole cities with all their inhabitants. The God of Jesus was a tender and loving God of forgiveness.

Here is an interesting comparison: *While the people of Israel were in the wilderness, they found a man gathering sticks on the sabbath day. And those who found him gathering sticks brought him to Moses and Aaron, and to all the congregation. . . . And the Lord said to Moses, "The man shall be put to death . . . ." And all the congregation brought him outside the camp, and stoned him to death with stones, as the Lord commanded*

Moses. (Num. 15:32-36)

And then 1500 years later: *One sabbath he was going through the grainfields; and as they made their way his disciples began to pluck heads of grain. And the Pharisees said to him, "Look, why are they doing what is not lawful on the sabbath?" And he said to them, "The sabbath was made for man, not man for the sabbath . . . ."* (Mark 2:23, 24, 27)

Little wonder that a child, studying the New Testament in Sunday school after a long period of Old Testament lessons, remarked, "Boy, God sure got better as He got older, didn't He?"

Unfortunately, much of our modern Christianity has held onto the God of the Old Testament, forsaking the God-concept of Jesus that was so meaningful and transcending. In all fairness it might be said that this is simply the result of a human tendency to define and visualize. Perhaps we can all identify with the little child who was crying in the dark in her room. Her mother came in to comfort her and said, "You needn't be afraid, for God is right here with you all the time."

"I know," sobbed the child, "but I want someone with skin on."

All through the centuries people have

attempted to depict and describe their divinity—the African fetish, the Egyptian dung-beetle, and cat-headed goddess; the Canaanite Baal, the Hindu Kali with her necklace of human skulls, and the all-too-human gods of the Greeks and Romans. Many of the symbols of the Christian church have their origin in this same tendency to find someone with "skin on." Here we find the saints, the figures of Jesus and Mary and the disciples, and angels and seraphim.

An eminent scientist stood looking at a modern painting of an angel, a gorgeous creature with wings that would outshine a peacock. Finally he said: "How can we expect our young people to come into the church when it implies believing in such anatomical monstrosities as that?"

While the Christian ideal has been centered around the concept of the worship of God, which usually means bowing before an altar, a statue, or a church official, Unity is concerned more with finding a consciousness of oneness with God, and then seeking to express God in thought, word, and act.

It would seem that those who insist on a type of worship that has God centered in places, things, and people, have missed one of the most revealing teachings of the entire Bible—Paul's immortal sermon on Mars' Hill: *"The God who made the world and everything in it, being Lord of heaven and earth, does not live in shrines made by man, nor is he served by human hands, as though he needed anything, since he himself gives to all men life and breath and everything.... Yet he is not far from each one of us, for 'In him we live and move and have our being....'"* (Acts 17:24-28)

We need to contemplate Jesus' saying that God is Spirit—the principle of life and intelligence, everywhere present at all times—just as accessible as the principle of mathematics and fully as free from formalism. Does the principle of mathematics give special attention to the blackboard that is gaily adorned and marked with fine figures? No, it works for all alike, impersonally. Neither does God care for forms and ceremonies, or ritual, or long and eloquent prayers. These things may have an influence upon the individual in helping him to feel a sense of communion, and to that extent certainly no one should say they are wrong. But we must remember that they have absolutely no influence on God.

What is God? Here we are faced with a

definition, which can only limit the limitless. We could say, God is Mind, God is Life, God is Substance, but whatever we agree God is, God is you. This may seem shocking to you, to think of yourself as God. But we did not say you are God. We said God is you. All ice is water, but not all water is ice. Whatever your life is, it is God. The life in you is God-life, the wisdom in you is God-intelligence, the love in you is God-love.

You are a child of God, an expression of God—so there can be nothing of you that is not innately of God. You are created as a perfect idea in God-Mind, and your purpose in life is to outpicture this idea in expression. There is no better way to worship God than to rightly express God.

A child was stretched out on the floor with paper and crayons. Her mother asked, "What are you drawing, dear?"

"I am drawing a picture of God," said the child.

"But no one knows what God looks like," replied the mother.

Dashing her crayon at the paper with abandon the child said, "They will when I get through."

This is our work, to outpicture God, to

fulfill God's likeness on earth "*. . . as it is in heaven.*" (Matt. 6:10) Jesus fully expressed God so that, in a sense, we can see what God looks like as we look at Him. *"He who has seen me has seen the Father . . . ."* (John 14:9)

This leads us quite naturally to consideration of Jesus. Jesus did not come to take the place of God, but rather to show people how they might find God for themselves and within themselves, even as Jesus Himself had found God within. There are whole libraries of books written about Jesus, about the mystical events surrounding His birth and life, about the prophetic hope that foretold His coming, about His miracles and teachings, and about the movement that has come into being in His name. But there is great confusion concerning the relationship between Jesus and Christ, which is the weakest link in the chain of Christian theology.

The Old Testament contains many prophecies concerning the coming of a Messiah. The hope of the prophet Isaiah many years before the birth of Jesus inspired him to proclaim: *For to us a child is born, to us a son is given; and the government will be upon his shoulder, and his name will be called "Wonderful Counselor, Mighty God, Everlasting Father,*

Prince of Peace." (Isa. 9:6)

Fundamental in traditional Christianity is the belief that this prophetic hope was fulfilled *in* Jesus, that Jesus is the hope of humankind for all time, that we must believe in Jesus to be saved. Unity teaches that this great hope was not fulfilled *in* Jesus but revealed *through* Him—and that the true hope of humankind is the Christ Spirit within the heart of every person, which Jesus in His illumined consciousness revealed. Paul writes: ... *Christ in you, the hope of glory.* (Col. 1:27)

Certainly Jesus is the Savior, the Way-Shower, the supreme revealer of Truth. But we miss the whole idea when we insist on worshiping Jesus, instead of following Him in the discovery of God within and the expression of the Christ.

Typical of the incorrect emphasis of Christian theology is John 3:16: *"For God so loved the world that he gave his only Son, that whoever believes in him should not perish but have eternal life."* This is used as proof that Jesus is the only Son of God. However, new light is given to this teaching by Meister Eckehart, one of the great Christian mystics of the Middle Ages through whom the "relentless stream of Truth" flowed easily. He wrote: *God never begot but one son, but the eternal is forever begetting the only begotten.* The "only Son" is spiritual man, the Christ principle, which is the divine spark within every person. Whoever believes in the Christ within, even as Jesus believed in the Christ in Himself, *should not perish but have eternal life.*

A key to understanding the teachings of Jesus is the discovery that Jesus did not place the emphasis on Himself, but always on *you,* your unfoldment, your believing, and your achievement. Jesus never claimed anything in the name of Jesus or the personal "me." He even said: *"If I bear witness to myself, my testimony is not true...."* (John 5:31) Yet He said, obviously speaking from the Christ consciousness: *"...he who believes in me will also do the works that I do; and greater works than these will he do...."* (John 14:12)

However, in John 12:44, He explains this by saying: *"He who believes in me, believes not in me but in him who sent me."* Thus, what He is really saying is, "Whoever believes in God in himself as I believe in God in me will do the works that I have done."

This is the keynote of Christianity. While

the Church has traditionally focused its attention and emphasis on Jesus, Jesus focuses His attention on you: "*. . . you also should do as I have done to you.*" (John 13:15) "*You, therefore, must be perfect, as your heavenly Father is perfect.*" (Matt. 5:48) "*You are the light of the world. . . . Let your light so shine . . . .*" (Matt. 5:14, 16)

If Jesus is held up to us as very God Himself, rather than the most perfect manifestation of God, if we preach that His purity is inimitable, that His unity with God cannot be repeated, then it all becomes unimportant and inconsequential, for what hope is there for you and me today?

But if we feel that the God to whom we pray is exactly the same God to whom Jesus prayed; that Jesus is flesh of our flesh and blood of our blood; that temptation and difficulty and suffering were real to Him; that there is no intimacy with the Father that He had which we cannot have (except the difference that he was the first to reach the Christ state and thusly we follow Him along that path); if we feel that He intended all humanity to realize perfect union with God—then life becomes a thrilling and hopeful experience, and Christianity becomes a tremendous practical guide to finding the life more abundant.

Charles Fillmore wrote: *He was more than Jesus of Nazareth, more than any other man who lived on earth. He was more than man, as we understand the appellation in its everyday use, because there came into His manhood a factor to which most men are strangers. This factor was the Christ consciousness. The unfoldment of this consciousness by Jesus made Him God incarnate, because Christ is the Mind of God individualized. We cannot separate Jesus Christ from God or tell where man leaves off and God begins in Him. To say that we are men as Jesus was a man is not exactly true, because He had dropped that personal consciousness by which we separate ourselves from our true God-self . . . He became consciously one with the absolute principle of Being. He proved in His resurrection and ascension that He had no consciousness separate from that of Being, therefore He really was this Being to all intents and purposes. Yet He attained no more than what is expected of every one of us. "That they may be one, even as we are one" was His prayer.*

Does Unity teach from the Bible? The answer is an emphatic "yes"! The Bible is

Unity's primary textbook. However, Unity insists upon a realistic approach to the Bible which takes it out of the realm of magic and superstition. One of the greatest limitations to understanding the Bible is the insistence on its infallibility. A thing is not true just because it is in the Bible. It is in the Bible because sometime through its long evolution certain people thought it contained material valuable in the quest for Truth. So, in a sense, we could say that it is not true because it is in the Bible; it is in the Bible because it is true. This is an important point.

The Bible was not handed down from the heavens in completed form, but was created. The sentences were constructed, the histories, stories, poems, proverbs, and prophecies were written. The Bible is essentially a record of human experiences in the quest for God and for Truth. But it must be recognized that this experience involves high points and low points. It shows the highest level of expression, and it shows the lowest and most human expression.

As a book of history the Bible is an important work; as a book of literature it is a jewel of literary power; and as a book of morals it has influenced all the legal codes of modern times. But if we stop here, we miss the whole idea, for in its literal acceptance it is full of inconsistencies and conflicting teachings.

Charles Fillmore said: *The Bible is, in its inner or spiritual meaning, a record of the experiences and the development of the human soul and of the whole being of man; also it is a treatise on man's relation to God, the creator and Father.*

Every human being commences in Adam, and within every human being lie the potentialities of Christ. The Bible expounds the nature of all the factors that make up human consciousness, all the conditions and states that taken together make up the sum of life, beginning with the lowest form of life, in Adam, and ending with the highest, in Christ. Between these two extremes lie all the stages of human development in orderly succession. Thus, with emphasis on you, the Bible actually becomes "the book of life."

Essentially, if we catch the true meaning of the Bible, it is prophetic and far-reaching, with the promise of overcoming, of regeneration, of resurrection and eternal life for *you.* One of the strange things is that religion has always tended toward retrospect—the backward look. In the time of Jesus, the Jewish religion of the day was a worship of the past, the God of Abraham, Isaac, and Jacob. The entire Hebrew theology dealt with the traditions, places, and people of days gone by. Jesus dared to translate the old into the new, to put this same religion into the present tense. He talked of salvation now, of the help of God at hand now, proving that the day of miracles is now: "... *the kingdom of heaven is at hand.*" (Matt. 4:17) For this He was called a blasphemer. For this He was considered a dangerous heretic and was crucified. All because He dared to teach that spiritual principles could be used by all people and that emphasis of true religion must be upon the individual, upon *you.*

Isn't it strange that Christianity, beginning with the impetus of Jesus, should have fallen right back into the same practice of worship in retrospect? How often we hear phrases like, "when God walked the earth" and "the age of miracles." Today, in answer to the question, "What is Unity?" we might say that Unity is daring to do what Jesus did in His day: to proclaim the practical aspect of spiritual principle, the livability of Christian teaching, the imminence of God and God-power. In other words, Unity is seeking only to put the teachings of Jesus in the present tense. Salvation now! Heaven now! God and healing power, present in you, now!

Unity is often criticized for making religion too easy. "You take away the ritual, the historic creeds, the Christian symbolism, the sacraments, the formal communion, the confessional, the church or priesthood as the intermediary between God and us, and what do you have left?" one might ask. The answer is, nothing but meditation and the study and application of Truth.

As for making religion too easy, Unity is probably the most difficult religious discipline in the world—simply because you are face-to-face with God and with yourself. There is nowhere to go, no one to blame, nothing to hide behind. You realize that your life experience is the result of your keeping of the law, that God can do no more for you than God can do through you, with the responsibility upon you of disciplining your thinking.

3

As a Man Thinketh

From the very beginning of human existence, we have been restless, curious, questioning beings. We have pondered the mystery of the stars above and the world around us. Like David of old, we have asked the question of ourselves and of life, "What are we?"

All the religions of the world and all the bibles of the world's religions are the outgrowth of this quest for Truth. All began with a spirit of restlessness and curiosity on the part of some individual that led to great discoveries in the realm of Spirit. Strangely enough, the history of religions reveals a common pattern: the crystallization of the first crystal-clear revelation, and the ultimate prohibition of further curiosity and questioning.

Religions have thus expected of their adherents something that it is not within the nature of many to give: the willingness to accept custom-made convictions about a defined and circumscribed world. For this reason the intellectuals and individualists of all time have rejected formal religion.

Christianity has followed this pattern of prohibiting a further quest for Truth or reality. For hundreds of years there was open warfare between the Christian church and those in science and philosophy. These scientists and philosophers were curious. They wanted to know "how" and "why." The church said, "Ours is not to reason why. Ours is to accept without question. To reason, to question, to analyze, is the path that leads to hell. Believe or be damned."

Fortunately there have always been those who were determined to "find out." The result of the courage of these people has led to the sciences of medicine, astronomy, mathematics, psychology, and many fields that today contribute to our modern way of life.

Witness the gradual progress of the mind of a little baby, and you see a miracle. What is the golden ladder on which the baby climbs out of mere consciousness into intelligence? Curiosity! As the child grows and matures he or she is confronted with a factor that comes into conflict with the innate spirit of curiosity: laziness and mental lethargy. Some people climb a little way up that ladder and then are satisfied. They would not open a new book, or stretch their minds in wonder at what lies even beyond the next desk above them, to say nothing of what lies beyond the stars, or what lies within themselves. Ceasing to be curious, they cease to grow as people. They begin to gravitate to a religious philosophy that provides them with a comfortable creed to accept and a religious life that is all worked out. For this reason, the many and varied denominations within Christianity all serve vital needs in the lives of those who are irresistibly drawn to their doctrine.

In answer to the question "What is Unity?" we might say here that Unity is an open door to self-discovery for those who are curious, who want to know more of the meaning of the world around and within them. Unity is a pathway to understanding for those who cannot accept final answers and precast spirituality, who feel the urge of curiosity, and who are willing to brave the scorn and ridicule of the passing throng, like Zaccheus, who climbed a tree to get a look at Jesus passing by. Some people may say of you as they probably said of Zaccheus, that you are way out on a limb in your spiritual seeking, but he saw the Christ and gained a wonderful awakening. So will you. Fortunately, as time goes on, more and more people are becoming open-minded about paths of self-discovery like Unity.

It is a great day in one's life when someone truly begins to discover himself. History is full of acts of those who discovered something of their capacities. As Emerson said: *Man is an inlet and may become an outlet of all there is in God.*

Walt Whitman realized this as he wrote: *There is no endowment in man or woman, that is not tallied in you. There is no virtue, no beauty in man or woman, but as good in you, no pluck, no endurance in others but as good in you.*

This is the divine spark, or the Christ within, that we referred to in the last chapter. It is the infinite possibility within us that we have the privilege and responsibility of releasing through the character of our thinking (or, to use a word that you will hear much in Unity and which will ultimately mean much to you) through *consciousness.*

One man brought his boss home to dinner. He had primed his precocious child to "be seen and not heard." The boss was a gruff and self-centered executive, a perfect caricature of the jokes made about bosses in general. The silenced lad stared at the boss through the evening. Finally, annoyed, the man asked, "Why do you keep looking at me that way?"

Seeing his father was out of the room, the boy broke the silence by saying, "My daddy says that you are a self-made man." The man beamed at this and proudly admitted that he had surely made his own way in the world, carving out his niche through hard work and ability. With candor the boy said, "But why did you make yourself like that?"

We all are constantly making ourselves what we are. Unity reveals that our lives and affairs are completely influenced and shaped by the character of our thinking, that a person is not limited by God's will or by heredity or environment or by fate or circumstance—

but by his own dominant state of mind. As Shakespeare voices it through one of his characters: *The fault, dear Brutus, is not in the stars, but in ourselves, that we are underlings.*

One of Unity's finest writers, Imelda Shanklin, says: *Your mind is your world. Your thoughts are the tools with which you carve your life story on the substance of the universe. When you rule your mind you rule your world. When you choose your thoughts you choose results. . . . Your life is what you think: Think straight, and life will become straight for you.*

Is this a startling idea to you? It should be startling, and even disturbing. It should shake you to the very foundation, for our lives are founded upon our dominant thought habits.

Someone might say: "But this is some strange notion of psychology or metaphysics. How do I know it is the truth? If thought is so important, why doesn't the Bible teach the power of constructive thinking?" That's just the point! The Bible teaches nothing else *but* this. It is not until we catch this underlying theme that the Bible begins to make sense.

Throughout the entire Old Testament, the

historical sequence, the teaching of the prophets, and the beauty of the Psalms, we find the intimation of that which Proverbs expresses tersely: *For as he* (man) *thinketh in his heart, so is he....* (Prov. 23:7, A.V.) Through parable and direct teaching Jesus stresses the importance of thought:... *Whatever a man sows* (in thought), *that he will also reap* (in his affairs). (Gal. 6:7) Jesus realized that the mind is the bridge between us, the finite, and the Infinite, and that even more than fervency and feeling in religion, the important element is our thoughts and attitudes. He said: *"... a man's foes will be those of his own household."* (Matt. 10:36) Jesus meant "the thoughts of his own mind." And Paul gives the *raison d'etre* of all religion when he says: *Do not be conformed to this world but be transformed by the renewal of your mind....* (Rom. 12:2)

In His parables of the "householder" and the "wise and unjust stewards," Jesus points to the truth that each person is ruler in the realm of mind, the master of his or her thoughts. Individuals may not be good masters, but they are masters. You cannot relinquish the responsibility. You may not have much power or authority in the world about you, and you may not be able to change or influence things to any great extent. But you have complete authority over what you think about these things.

All too many of us think that being possessed by any thought that chances to come along is unavoidable. It may be a matter of regret that we have been awake all night worrying about some problem in our lives, but we tell about it as if it were something over which we have no control. We have yet to discover that we have the power to determine whether or not we are going to be kept awake, whether or not we are going to worry. We may not realize it, but we worry because we make the decision that this is the way we determine to face our problem. Always there is a choice. "... *Choose this day whom you will serve* ...." (Josh. 24:15)

If a pebble in our shoe torments us, we stop in our tracks and do something about it. We take off the shoe and shake it out. Once the matter is understood, it is just as easy to expel an intruding and obnoxious thought from the mind.

Robert A. Millikan, the great physicist, said: *In the final analysis, the thing in this world which is of most supreme importance, indeed the thing which is of most practical value to the race, is not, after all, useful discovery or invention, but that which lies far back of them, namely, the way men think.*

Charles Fillmore was even more dramatic and emphatic: *God's greatest gift to man is the power of thought, through which he can incorporate into his consciousness the Mind of God.*

The Unity teaching clearly identifies thought as the coin of the spiritual realm. Religion notwithstanding, there is no substitute for good, creative, positive thinking. It is the absence of positive thinking that is at the root of the age-old dilemma of the Christian: "Why should a good Christian person suffer so?" But what is a "good Christian"? One who supports the church, keeps its holy days, and gives assent to all its theology? This is good, but it is not enough. The true Christian is the one who, as was once said: *lets that same mind that was in Christ Jesus be in him,* and who thinks in tune with God in the same positive and constructive way that Jesus did. The purpose of the Christian church is not to make you a convert to a particular creed and a member of a particular organization. The true purpose of Christianity is to help you to, as was said in Romans, *be transformed by the renewal of your mind.*

The best possible method of thought training is prayer. Unfortunately, the moment we mention the word "prayer" we are at the mercy of the thousand and one connotations of the word that are held by people. Prayer is undoubtedly the most misunderstood facet of Christianity. Prayer is thought of as intrinsically invariable. It is grouped with such definite actions as to walk, to breathe, to talk. We overlook the fact that there is the question of where we walk, how we breathe, what we say.

Contemporary Christian prayer is largely a modification of the prayer concepts of pre-Christian days, a plea to a superman sort of God somewhere off in the skies. It is usually a wordy and emotional plea to God to have mercy, along with a reminder that He is omnipotent.

In many cases prayer is simply a form of words, a ritual, a custom that is followed— that which usually involves outer practice and ceremony more than inner feeling and sincerity. It is a practice that often has lost its meaning but not its place in everyday life.

It is said that the Hawaiians were a praying people long before the Christian missionaries brought the new religion to them. The Hawaiian worshiper used to sit outside the Temple for a long time meditating and preparing before entering. And after going to his altar he would again sit a long time outside, this time to "breathe life" into his prayers. The Hawaiians noted that the Christians, when they came, just got up, uttered a few sentences, said "Amen," and were done. For this reason they were called *haolis* which means "without breath"—those who fail to breathe life into their prayers.

When we think of God as Spirit, and of ourselves as the expression of God, then we can understand what Jesus meant when He said: "*. . . your Father knows what you need before you ask him.*" (Matt. 6:8) Prayer, then, is not for God at all. It is for us. Startling as it may sound, it really doesn't make any difference to God whether or not we pray, *but it makes a lot of difference to us.* Prayer is not a matter of conquering God's reluctance, but of attuning ourselves to God's eternal willingness.

One thing is certain: When we pray we do not stop thinking. The mind is the connecting link between God and us. If prayer is anything, it is high-level, creative thinking. Emerson says: *Prayer is the contemplation of the facts of life from the highest point of view.*

All the powers of heaven and earth cannot help us unless they help us to change or control our thought, for as you think in your heart, that is what you are. If lack is your problem, God cannot help you or prosper you—even if you secure the help of all the praying people in the world—until you change your thought of lack. Prayer will help you to change your thought from that of lack to the realization of your all-sufficiency in all things. Once you begin to think "abundance," the flow of supply will pour out upon you. Paul says: *And my God will supply every need of yours according to his riches* .... (Phil. 4:19) God always supplies your needs, but God cannot fill your lack—because lack is not an experience but a negative thought. Change the thought and you change the experience.

Unity teaches the prayer of affirmation. It is not begging or asking, but claiming and accepting. Not "I want," "I wish," "I hope," "I desire," but "I AM." Not "help me," "guide me," "heal me," "prosper me," but "I AM now helped and guided and healed and prospered." The prophet Joel once declared: *. . . let the weak say, I am strong.* (Joel 3:10, A.V.) This is the secret of affirmative prayer. If there is a need, instead of dwelling in thought on the need, claim the truth—speak the word. All that you need or desire you already have in the kingdom of your inner potential. And Jesus said: ". . . *it is your Father's good pleasure to give you the kingdom.*" (Luke 12:32)

The entire Unity teaching might well be summed up under the headings of "prayer" and "right thinking." This might seem to be an easy sort of religion. However, it is a most difficult religious discipline, just because it is a discipline. Jesus said: ". . . *you will know the truth, and the truth will make you free.*" (John 8:32) This implies the discipline of *knowing* the truth and not just knowing about it.

What is this freedom that Jesus brought to humankind? Many have thought of it as a freedom from concern over salvation, a sense of being "saved" for all time through joining a church or giving assent to a religious creed. There is no final salvation. It is a day-by-day process to discipline thought and action. Unity is "practical Christianity," and it is practical only if it is practiced. *And* practice means regular and disciplined effort. Every time you make the effort to meet life with a positive thought, you are "saved" from the inevitable effect of negative thought.

Sometimes people deeply desire a strong, healthy, and physically fit body, but will not spend the time and energy to exercise and eat right. Instead, they overeat, drink to excess, and smoke, only wishing for total physical health.

So it is with the spiritual life. There is no intermediary between God and you but your own mind. There is no way into the kingdom of healthy, happy, and prosperous living except through your own disciplined effort.

Unity presents workable techniques in the demonstration of Jesus' teachings, but they will require faithful and disciplined practice. Reading Unity books or attending Unity lectures will not create for you that intangible something called "consciousness" any more than reading a book about golf will make you a good golfer.

How much time should one spend in the "practice of the presence of God"? All the time! The law is, "You are what you think." We are constantly thinking, and our thoughts are constantly influencing our lives for good or ill. You can't help thinking because you are a thinking being. You might as well learn to think right, and right thinking is prayer. Become a positive thinker and *pray constantly.* (I Thess. 5:17)

4

Working with Workable Law

We live today in a changing world. Religion for today must be well suited to meet the needs of these times. One of the weaknesses of traditional Christianity has been the determination to present Jesus' teachings in the idiom and symbol appropriate to His time, but inappropriate to the very conditions of our time. If Jesus came into our world today, He would express Himself in ways that meet head-on the needs of this modern technological age. Thus, Christianity, to be practical and effective, must be constantly reinterpreted to each succeeding generation in terms of vital significance to that generation's thought.

Several years ago, LIFE magazine commented editorially on the giant strides being made by science into unknown territory: *It would seem that the more we learn about Life and the Universe the more of an enigma they become from the viewpoint of science, if science limits itself to the "how" of things. Only when it includes a "why," that which is beyond the scope of the laboratory bench, is it possible for any rhyme or reason to appear in its accumulated knowledge.*

The editorial continued: *Modern metaphysics is no longer irrelevant to science but indispensable to it if a total picture is to be achieved. In fact, metaphysics, by taking cognizance of the latest advances in science, could become man's greatest quest during the next hundred years.*

This is where Unity stands. Unity is a form of Christian metaphysics, a modern interpretation of the Christian teaching with insight into the world of today, and vision for the world of tomorrow.

Marcus Bach, one of America's leading authorities in the field of contemporary religious movements, said in an article published a few years ago: *No modern religious movement has made more of an impact upon American faith than Unity. We in the traditional churches have been strong in our knowing. Unity is strong in its doing, its know-how. We talk about holy habits and spiritual exercises, but what we desperately need is to apply ourselves to the actual doing thereof.*

Unity is a study of the teachings of Jesus Christ, free from the influence of theology, and with an open mind. Among the fundamentals of Jesus' teachings is one idea so dynamic in its implications that it should be shouted from the housetops. When this message gets into the consciousness of humankind, we will be done with fear and worry forever, for we will have the key to faith. When we fully know this message, we will never again accept anything as impossible or incurable. We will never lose hope. We will work by all the means at our command to achieve the health and well-being that we desire, and even more, we will command the means, for we will realize that we have resources within that are limitless.

What is this message? *The kingdom of God is within you.* The right understanding of this message will change many traditional concepts about the afterlife. Most important, however, it will reveal that *within you is the unborn possibility of limitless experience, and yours is the privilege of giving birth to it.*

Thus, the keynote of the Unity teaching is that all of us contain an individual portion of the original creative force of the universe, and by conscious direction of will can open ourselves to and receive its power.

It is unfortunate but true that through the ages theologians devoted so much time to trying to find and analyze the body of God that they lost the consciousness of God's imminence and dynamic power. Because they placed the emphasis on the miracles wrought by Jesus and the worship of His personality, they lost sight of the fact that He was simply demonstrating the possibility of universal principle and the power of the Christ indwelling.

We live in a universe of law. Unity is not a theology, but a study of spiritual law—the same spiritual law that enabled Jesus to do the great works attributed to Him. Jesus said: *Think not that I am come to destroy the law ... I am not come to destroy, but to fulfil.* (Matt. 5:17, A.V.) We misunderstand His mission and His teaching when we think of

His work as an abolishment of divine law. Jesus simply revealed a higher potential of divine law than as yet humankind is aware of. There is no special law for anyone, not even for Jesus; but anyone can specialize the law by using it with fuller understanding.

We can never really understand the truth of Jesus Christ until we give up once and for all the idea of caprice or favoritism in the universe, and until we cease to pray to receive without giving or to be forgiven when we have not changed our attitudes. So long as we believe in a God who interferes with nature to please someone who has asked a favor, we will not have a strength of faith upon which to build our lives.

The Unity ideal of practical Christianity deals with the study of spiritual law and its influence in our lives and affairs. Unity believes that when Jesus said: "... *I came that they might have life, and have it abundantly,*" (John 10:10) He meant what He said. Unity teaches that it is not only possible to demonstrate health and prosperity in our lives today, but it is our duty to continually press on to a greater awareness of God and a greater demonstration of His good in mind, body, and affairs.

There is increasingly widespread interest today in spiritual healing. Often it is a looking for the magical, the mystical, and the miraculous. Unity teaches spiritual healing, and Unity students have reported some unusual and near-miraculous results. However, Unity teaches that spiritual healing is not feasible simply because of intercession with God or through some special dispensation of divine law. Spiritual healing is possible because we are spiritual beings, because the kingdom of God is within.

For some strange reason that is not found in Jesus' teaching, the Christian teaching has insisted that sickness is the will of God and should be passively accepted. The church has limited its ministrations to "comfort for the afflicted," giving moral courage to endure that which most surely is "God's will." Unity teaches that sickness is never the will of God, that God is Spirit, the very essence of life, and that this essence could not be working against itself.

In Ezekiel we read: *Cast away from you all the transgressions which you have committed against me, and get yourselves a new heart and a new spirit! Why will you die . . . . For I have no pleasure in the death of any one, says the Lord God; so turn, and live.*" (Ezek. 18:31, 32) Today Unity is dedicated to this message: "*. . . so turn, and live.*"

Jesus did not originate spiritual healing. He did not create the healing law. He simply discovered and brought to full flower the great Truth of the healing principle by which anyone may rise above sickness or weakness into perfect life and wholeness. This healing principle is God in action. It is not something extraneous to us that acts upon us when properly contacted. In the largest sense the "healing principle" is our very life itself.

Charles Fillmore writes: *Health, real health, is from within and does not have to be manufactured in the without. It is the normal condition of man, a condition true to the reality of his being.* Healing is normal; it is God's will. Working for health does not mean fighting a force of sickness. There is only one force—God. You are an expression of God, containing the potential of perfect life. There is nothing in God that could or would limit your life. There is no law of sickness. You experience sickness because in your consciousness you have limited the expression of that perfect life.

In this matter of spiritual healing it is well

to clarify Unity's ideal: *There is only one healing power.* There cannot really be a human *and* a divine cure. All healing is divine.

The Unity teachings regarding spiritual healing are not points of doctrine that the individual must accept or be dropped from the rolls. No one will ever be condemned or ridiculed for turning to medical or surgical help in the occurrence of health problems. Unity has no resistance to doctors or the field of medicine. As a matter of fact, Unity recognizes the invaluable service to humanity that the science of medicine is rendering in alleviating suffering and prolonging life.

Unity does not consider its efforts as being opposed to those of medical practice, nor would a Unity counselor or minister refuse to work spiritually with one who is at the same time being treated medically. I once stood holding the left hand of a critically ill patient, praying for the release of healing life—while a young physician administered a hypodermic injection in the right arm. Later the doctor said that something wonderful happened in those few moments, and, he said, "It was bigger than both of us."

More and more doctors are recognizing that the inner healing power of the body is not strictly a material thing, a power that can be expressed in terms of hemoglobin and white corpuscles, but a spiritual power of which the action of these are but symptoms. Sometimes it seems that physicians have a greater faith in the healing principle within than do some ministers.

Too much faith in the doctor is wrong, simply because we allow him to become a crutch. But too much faith in a spiritual healer is wrong for the same reason. The problem is not in any inherent evil in drugs and medicines and medical techniques. It is in letting them become the object of our faith, which should be placed in God.

Unity teaches the pathway of health through spiritual means. It stresses the importance of progressing to the place where we can put our hand in the hand of God and depend on God only. But there should be no condemnation of ourselves or others if it seems necessary to crawl before we walk. Unity does not insist that you go all the way in spiritual healing. It urges you to go as far as you can on faith—and you will be amazed at how far you can go.

Unity also teaches the prosperity law, the law of abundance. But Unity is no get-rich-

quick scheme. Neither does it promise something for nothing in "ten easy lessons." Life
is governed by certain changeless spiritual
and natural laws which cannot be altered or
abolished to fit selfish whims. However,
when you understand the law and work within it, you not only begin to draw prosperity
and success to you, but you can't keep them
away. Unity is a study of these unfailing
laws.

In this limitless universe there is a royal
abundance of all good. There is sunlight for
all, there is air for all, there is life for all. *You
shall remember the Lord your God, for it is he
who gives you power to get wealth . . . .* (Deut.
8:18)

The promise is: ". . . *seek his kingdom, and
these things shall be yours as well.*" (Luke
12:31) Prosperity and success will come easily and freely when you look to God as the
source of your good and give thanks that
within yourself is the unborn possibility of
opulence and fulfillment. We need to condition our minds to receive and express this
infinite possibility by affirming: *I am a rich
and healthy and dynamic child of God. I
think rich and healthy thoughts, and I expect
rich and healthy results.*

Just a word here in answer to the critics of the concept of practical Christianity. It is strange but true that long-faced Christians have always resisted the concept of using Christianity for other than the resigned acceptance of life's experiences as God's will. One critic in a national magazine recently derided what he called, "the concept of God for hire." He makes a statement that we hear often in fundamental Christianity but which never ceases to amaze a student of Truth: *Faith in God and optimism may help us withstand our problems, but they can't solve them.* This is a strange philosophy passing for Christianity, and it certainly did not originate with Jesus.

The critic says "let's stop misusing God," but he infers that to use God at all is to misuse God. What of the tree in your yard? Does it not use the forces of nature? Is it wrong for the tree to draw upon the abundance of nature in order to flourish with green leaves and fragrant blossoms and fruitage? Didn't Jesus say: "... *Consider the lilies of the field, how they grow ... yet I tell you, even Solomon in all his glory was not arrayed like one of these.*" (Matt. 6:28, 29)

As expressions of God, we "use God" every

moment. When we cast about for an idea and say, "I have it," where did this idea come from? Is there not but one Mind? The thoughts of our minds, the love of our hearts, the life of our bodies, and the substance of our affairs—all are the essence of God that we use in living.

The old idea that prevails with traditionalists is a God who sits up in the skies, who grants favors and brings punishment. To turn to God in "prayer" by begging for various needs is to misuse God. However, Jesus said: *"God is spirit, and those who worship him must worship in spirit and truth."* (John 4:24) God is the life principle, the prospering principle. Continued use of a principle in no way depletes the principle. Every time you work a problem in mathematics you "use" the principle. There is no other way to find the answer. If every man, woman, and child in the world were to add two plus two at the same time there would be not even the slightest depletion of the principle. All would easily arrive at the answer—four. And there is no depletion of God through our practice of God's presence or demonstration of divine law.

Unity teaches that God is Spirit as Jesus

taught that God is Spirit. Unity seeks to understand and to demonstrate the workable law of Spirit as Jesus understood and worked with workable law. Unity teaches as Jesus taught, that: "... *All things are possible to him who believes.*" (Mark 9:23) And: "... *whatever you ask in prayer, you will receive, if you have faith.*" (Matt. 21:22)

5

The Perfect Round

Through the ages there have been many philosophies of the heretofore and the hereafter. People have forever been searching their souls and the world about them for answers to such questions as: "Why am I here? Where am I going? Why am I like I am?"

The atheist might say, "This is all there is. You are like the tree or animal. You came into life because the seed was planted. You leave this life if and when life is either accidentally or naturally taken from you. You only live once. Enjoy yourself."

The religious concepts of life are too numerous to mention. They all, however, have believed in this life as only a part of the whole. They all have believed in a soul and its survival of death. From there they branch out into the hundreds of doctrinal beliefs and shades of meaning within those beliefs.

The afterlife concept of heaven is a carry-over of the early heathen belief of the "happy hunting ground." The vague feelings of the continuity of life beyond death have forever haunted the souls of humankind. This has been made complex with the idea that there are two divergent paths. One is up and the other down—the happy place reserved only for the good, while the rest suffer eternal torment.

This has been largely the Christian concept. However, it leaves many unanswered questions: If this life is but the preparation for something to come, why are we not anxious to get into the next life? How do we account for the inbred desire to live? How do we account for the seemingly unfinished pattern of the individual lives and the constantly progressive patterns of civilization?

Unity is not in itself an answer to all these questions. It is, rather, a challenge to keep asking them. Unity does suggest answers. But it will tell you again and again that the final answer must come from within yourself.

To find an adequate understanding of life, we must realize that it cannot be comprehended in terms of the brief span of years that begins with birth and ends with death. We have thought of life as a passing experience. We have said, when someone meets an unfortunate experience, "Well, that's life for you." But it is not life at all. It is a poor imitation, a restriction of the meaning and power of life.

We have been taught to think that life is ever on the ebb, that time is running out, and that though we may work ever so hard to stave it off, emptiness, sickness, lack, deterioration, and death are ultimates—foreordained from the start. We say, "For a woman of her age she does pretty well; after all, life does take its toll." But life takes no toll at all. There is no penalty or premium.

Often when someone is meeting a challenging experience, we say, "You need to get a new hold on life." Why? Life won't run off and leave you. Life has hold of *you*. Actually, you do not live life; life lives you. It animates you, and expresses itself *as* you. It is living you this moment. It will never let you go.

Robert Browning gives insight into the problem of life when he writes: *On the earth, the broken arcs; in the heaven, the perfect round.*

Can you comprehend the complete circle if one tiny segment of a circle is presented to you? If this segment is so small as to be little more than a dot on the paper, there is no way of determining whether it is of a tiny circle or a circle the size of the earth. And yet if it *is* a segment of a circle, it is *always* a segment that can be understood only in terms of the whole circle. In the same sense we can only understand life in terms of one's completion as a spiritual being—that which is not limited to or by the physical body.

Undoubtedly all of us have at some time been exposed to a theology that presented the blood and thunder of God and the hereafter. God was a stern and unrelenting judge, who sat on a throne somewhere and recorded in a big book all the deeds of our lives. The story includes a final "judgment" when the books are balanced, and if the balance is found to be in our favor we go up, and if against, we go down. We have envisioned heaven with angels and harps and white billowy clouds, and the domain of hell with its hot furnaces, its mass of people writhing in everlasting torment.

Sensible people have always rejected this ridiculous picture. It seems inconceivable that intelligent people could admit to such a capricious and sadistic deity that would allow or direct such things. In the words of poet Arlington Robinson: *The world of religious thought and life has ever been a kind of spiritual kindergarten in which millions of bewildered infants are trying to spell "God" with the wrong blocks.*

In his book, "East and West," Sri Radhakrishnan says: *The doctrine of hell-fire is inconsistent with Jesus' life and teaching. Jesus asks us to forgive our brethren even if they sin against us "seventy times seven." If He expects us to behave in this way, God cannot be different. There must be something undivine in God, if He is responsible for everlasting hell-fire.*

The "hellfire" theory holds that all pagans, heathens, and non-Christians of every description are excluded from heaven and thus consigned to hell if they die in their benighted state. Just imagine, if your imagination can compass or tolerate so awful an idea: sixteen hundred million souls in this generation alone, and no less than one hundred billion sentient beings wallowing in eternal fire since the awakening of man in the last four thousand years. A universe that could permit or cause so monstrous a thing would be worse than worthless from every standpoint.

The word *hades,* which is usually erroneously translated "hell" in the Bible, comes from a root word which means "not to see." It means a state of being unable to see the good. Heaven, then, would mean a state of clear seeing. It is written of Jesus on several instances when He was faced with challenging needs: ... *he lifted up his eyes to heaven* .... (John 17:1) He turned from the facts of human need to the truth of God's all-sufficiency. He turned from "not seeing" to "clear seeing," from hell to heaven. There is little question of it, there is a lot of hell in life, but it is hell that we make ourselves by wrong seeing and thinking.

The great need is not to *set* things right, but to *see* them rightly—and Christianity is a passport from illusion to reality. This is the role of Unity. Unity is not trying to change people or the world by social action or any other outer means. It is seeking only to see things rightly and to help people to see things rightly. It seeks to help people to see good beyond appearances of evil, to see strength beyond weakness and answers within answers. Jesus said: *"Do not judge by appearances, but judge with right judgment."* (John 7:24)

Jesus placed great emphasis on the mystical something that He called "heaven." He talked about it often and usually in parables. Had the kingdom of heaven been off in the skies, a city with golden streets, He could easily have located it that way. Yet He said: *"The kingdom of heaven is like a grain of mustard seed. . . . The kingdom of heaven is like leaven. . . .* (Matt. 13:31, 33) Strange comparisons if He had in mind a place where the good go after death. Finally, He said: *"The kingdom of God is not coming with signs to be observed; nor will they say, 'Lo, here it is!' or 'There!' for behold, the kingdom of God is in the midst of you."* (Luke 17:20, 21)

It seems obvious that Jesus' kingdom of God or of heaven refers to an unseen and yet very real phase of life rather than a place associated only with death. The word *heaven* comes from the Greek word *ouranos* which means "expanding." Certainly Jesus' parables about heaven seem to point to the miracle of growth in growing things. Heaven, then, is that wonderful germ of possibility that lies within all of God's creation. It is the perfect circle within the broken arc. It is the potential for perfect health and happiness within sickness and heartache and failure.

The kingdom of God is a substance or life or mind-essence which is at the root of all things, the primal substance of which all things are made. It is not life or force as we recognize it, but something much more concentrated than that. It is the conception of life and primal substance as the sum of all its undistributed powers, being as yet none of these in particular, but all of them in potentiality. Now we see why Jesus had to use parables to teach such an abstract idea.

Because we have always associated heaven and hell with an afterlife, we may now wonder, what about immortality? What takes place "beyond the sunset" of earthly life? First of all, let us remember that we do not have to die to be immortal. We are immortal here and now. Jesus talked much about immortality and eternity, but we have missed His meaning because we have been thinking in terms of time and space, of when and where. Jesus is not talking about that which is to be, but that which now is.

In John 5:24 Jesus said: "*. . . he who hears my word and believes him who sent me, has eternal life; he does not come into judgment, but has passed from death to life.*" Not "will have" but "has"! When you hear Truth and believe it, when it becomes part of your consciousness, you suddenly come to life for the first time. Your eyes are opened and you see things and people in depth. You are aware of a new dimension of life that reveals meaning and purpose to all things.

We are amphibious, living in two worlds, not in succession but concurrently—two worlds which are yet one. We are spiritual beings, living in a spiritual world, governed by spiritual law. But we are also clothed in human form, moving through human experience. We live in preoccupation with the physical and material, but as Ecclesiastes tells us: *. . . he has put eternity into man's mind. . . .* (Eccles. 3:11) At any time we can perceive the depth and breadth and the infinite resources of life in the dimension of eternity.

You may now be thinking, "all this notwithstanding, the fact is that people do die and life does seem to end. What of the fact of death?'' There has always been an instinctive belief in the immortality of the soul, in a life that goes on in some way after death. Death has always been the unanswered question, for the startling truth is, no one has ever seen death! We see only what it has no further use for, what it leaves behind.

One of our problems in achieving a spiritually oriented understanding of life is that most of us are body-centered rather than soul-centered. We may give intellectual assent to the idea of the soul, but we refer to it as something that is added to our nature. We may say, ''I have a soul.'' But you do not have a soul at all, strange as that may sound. You *are* a soul, and your soul *has* a body.

Certain erroneous Christian doctrines have talked vaguely of the possibility of losing your soul. How can you lose what you are? Your soul is your one eternal identity. It is the facet of God-life which is your privilege and responsibility to express and perfect.

The physical body is a marvelously created and sustained expression of life, truly ''the temple of the living God.'' However, it is not the center of your life, but simply the means of its outward expression. If the body is rendered unfit for further service, if it succumbs to the race beliefs of sickness, age, and deterioration, and is thereby laid aside, this in no way means that life for you has ended. It simply means that you, as a living soul, will move from one room into another in the Father's house which Jesus assures us has many rooms.

In our modern funeral customs we find a strange mixture of pagan practices and confused religious ideals. The practice of embalming the body and putting it on display comes to us from the early Egyptian concept of the worship of the dead. The time must come when Christians will accept the idea of "let the dead bury the dead," when the garment of the flesh will be carefully and lovingly disposed of through cremation, and when the funeral service will be a simple time of prayer for the guidance of the loved one who goes forth into a new experience, and for the strength and comfort of those who remain.

The fact of death presents many problems to the sincere student of religion. How do we account for all that seems so unfinished, so incomplete, on the one hand, and Jesus' command, "*You, therefore, must be perfect...*" (Matt. 5:48) on the other? This is the eternal call to ... *press on toward the goal for the prize of the upward call of God in Christ Jesus.* (Phil. 3:14) How can we justify the fact that so many souls are born and live out their lives in mediocrity and unfulfillment? Obviously Jesus would not have given the command, if there were no means by which it could and should be fulfilled.

How do we account for the seeming inequality in life? Are we all supposed to reach the same height even though we start on different levels? We are told that all people are created equal, that all are children of God. So how can we justify the fact that some are born in perfect health while others are born crippled, deformed, or blind? Is God then not a God of fairness and justice?

Unity suggests an answer: the theory of reincarnation. Unfortunately, the idea of reincarnation has been ridiculed due to misunderstanding and misinformation. Charles Fillmore says: *When man loses his body by death, the law of expression works within him for re-embodiment .... Divine mercy permits this process in order that man may have further opportunity to demonstrate Christ life. But generation and death must give place to regeneration and eternal life. The necessity of rebirth must, therefore, pass away with all other makeshifts of the mortal man. It will have no place when men take advantage of the redeeming, regenerating life of Christ and quit dying.*

Death is not in the plan of God, but in human consciousness. We are born to live and not to die. In the apocryphal book, "The Wisdom of Solomon," we read: *Court not death in the error of your life; neither draw upon yourselves destruction by the works of your hands; because God made not death; neither delighteth he when the living perish; for he created all things that they might have being; and the generative powers of the world are healthsome, and there is no poison of destruction in them: nor hath hades royal dominion on earth, for righteousness is immortal.*

In a sense the concept of reincarnation might be called "the gospel of the second chance." Even though one might die, through the forgiveness of God he or she is given another opportunity to press on toward the ultimate goal of perfection through reembodiment. However, let us make this clear: this is no fixed doctrine of Unity. It is simply a glorious possibility. Unity suggests it as an answer to the many puzzling questions that arise about death. If the idea does not appeal to you, or if it frightens you, forget it. Put it out of your mind. More important is what you think and how you live today.

It is often asked, "If reincarnation is true, why isn't it mentioned in the Bible?" Actually it is, but its direct allusions are few and are quite subtle. It would seem that the belief was so common that it is taken for granted. For instance, Jesus asked the disciples: *"Who do men say that the Son of man is?"* (Matt. 16:13) Their reply was: *"Some say John the Baptist, others say Elijah, and others Jeremiah or one of the prophets."* (Matt. 16:14) Their reply would seem to indicate that the idea of reincarnation prevailed among the people.

Perhaps the clearest allusion is in the ninth chapter of John, in the case of the man born blind. The disciples are puzzled about the reason for a man's having been born blind. They asked: *". . . who sinned, this man or his parents, that he was born blind?"* (John 9:2) How could he have caused his own blindness by sin if he was born blind? Obviously the question reflects a clear allusion to a previous life. It shows that the belief did prevail. And

Jesus' answer indicated that both theories were reasonable, because he did not reject or ridicule them. He simply stated that they did not apply in this case: "*It was not that this man sinned, or his parents, but that the works of God might be made manifest in him.*" (John 9:3)

In other words, the affliction was simply a means of working out something that, according to the consciousness of the individual, could not be worked out in any other way. This is a good answer for the puzzling question we often ask of life, "Why did this happen to me?" Despite the law of cause and effect, challenging experiences are not always the negative results of negative causes. When we see a student challenged to the utmost with the tests that are daily presented in courses of study, do we wonder what could have caused this terrible thing? No. We realize that it is for the purpose of the student's own growth and development.

Looking at the challenge of blindness from the end rather than the beginning of life, do we ask in the case of Helen Keller, "What could have caused so tragic a thing to happen? Who sinned, this woman or her parents?" We do not question thusly, because

we see that the works of God have been
manifest in her. We realize that she has
achieved the stature of her life not in spite of
her blindness but actually because of it.
Somehow, in the ongoing of the great soul,
that which she wanted to unfold could seemingly have been accomplished in no other
way.

It is good to constantly seek to improve
ourselves and our manner of thinking. But
more important than why things have come
to us is the question of what we are going to
do about them, how we gain strength and
stature in rising above them.

As concerns the concept of reincarnation, it
may give some satisfying answers to life's
urgent questions. But do not make it an object of study. Reincarnation is not a goal in
life, but only a blessed means of going on in
spite of death, which Paul says is the *wages
of sin . . . .* (Rom. 6:23) There are countless
"authorities" who will give you "authentic"
facts about reincarnation, when it takes
place, and how and to whom you will return
to earth after death. For a "price" there
are also those who will tell you that in previous lives you were the Queen of Sheba or a
knight of the Round Table. (It is strange and

perhaps significant that you are never told that you were a peasant or slave.) Shun these so-called investigations. They can only serve to confuse you and to keep you from the main goal of spiritual seeking—which is an understanding of life, not death.

Through all the Unity teachings you will find the emphasis on the here and now. Unity will constantly challenge you to live today as if it were the only day of your life. *This is the day which the Lord has made; let us rejoice and be glad in it.* (Psalms 118:24)

6

Techniques for
Abundant Living

Unity is not simply a church to join or a creed to espouse. Unity is a study of religion as a science of living. It is an interpretation of the teachings of Jesus Christ with prime emphasis on practice. Obviously it will hold no interest for those whose religion is a white cloak to be wrapped around them on Sunday morning and then tossed into the six-day closet of unconcern.

Essentially Unity is a technique in realizing the abundant life. It consists of thoughts to think, words to speak, positive and creative things to do. Following are some simple yet practical things that you may find helpful. They are given here as a sample of Unity's emphasis on the practical. These techniques for abundant living are not simply to read, but to affirm and decree in the face of challenging times. They will work for you, if you work for them.

Meeting Change

The one real certainty in life is change. Because of our desire for stability and security, sometimes we resist and become anxious during changing conditions. We need to prayerfully build into our consciousness the realization that: *The eternal God is your dwelling place, and underneath are the everlasting arms.* (Deut. 33:27)

Affirm: I do not resist change, for I know that only God, the good, governs me, my circumstances, my environment.

Reflect: God gives me the wisdom and strength to meet the inevitable changes that occur in my life. I meet them easily and lovingly. I may not see how changes can be a blessing, but I keep my thoughts loving,

positive, and fearless. Not only has God prepared the way before me, but God has prepared me, readied me to meet each phase of
life as it unfolds before me. Spirit fills me
with the faith to know that all my affairs are
working together for good.

Forgiveness

One of the greatest stumbling blocks for
many people is forgiveness of wrong-doers, or
self-forgiveness and accepting the forgiveness of God. This affirmation will help you to
enter into the current of divine love and let its
forgiving activity flow freely through you:

Affirm: The forgiving love of God sets me
free, and I am at peace.

Reflect: The forgiving love of God now fills
my heart and floods my entire being. I let go
any thought that others have injured me in
any way. I let go every feeling of bitterness
and resentment. I am now free from the belief
that other persons can be responsible for
unpleasant conditions that may exist in my
life. I am filled with love, and I am at peace. I
now see myself in the light of God's love in

me that reveals my deepest strengths and my highest ideals. I now forgive myself for past mistakes and open my mind and heart to the activity of God's love that frees me from feelings of guilt and helps me to know that my understanding grows with every experience. I am now open and receptive and responsive to the forgiving love of God. I am at peace. I am free.

Prosperity

We live in an opulent universe. Supply and success are our rightful inheritance. Prosperity manifests, not by asking God for more, but by conditioning our minds through prayer to accept more of God's good.

Affirm: God is my all-sufficient resource, my instant, constant, and abundant supply.

Reflect: God is my supply, everywhere evenly present, and as immediately available as the air I breathe. The moment a need arises in my life, God's infinite substance is immediately at hand to fill it. I am a child of God, and it is right and good that I manifest abundance. As God's child, I have been given the wisdom and intelligence to bring into expression all that is needed for my well-being and comfort. God inspires me with good judgment in handling the supply that is already mine, and opens the way to greater good, greater blessings, greater opportunities.

Healing

The Twenty-third Psalm is one of the loveliest poems in all literature. It is spoken in the language of a shepherd, but it easily translates into the language of our experience and need. To the one who is meeting a healing challenge it could have this faith-inspired meaning:

Affirm: The Lord is my health, I can't be sick. He makes me to relax from all tension; He leads me into peace of mind and heart, He restores my zest for living. He guides me into using my body wisely for His name's sake. Yea, though I am surrounded by disease and the thought of disease, I will have no fear, for You are with me. Your truth and life sustain me. You prepare a reserve within me to meet all life's challenges; You charge my heart with healing life. My energy is unbounded.

Surely health and joy shall follow me all the days of my life; and I will dwell in the consciousness of wholeness forever.

Healing the Heart

An expression commonly used by spiritual-minded people is "Bless your heart!" It conveys the implication that if your heart is blessed, your life will be harmonious and whole. Let us bless the organ called your heart.

Affirm: I am one with the one great Heart that beats for all.

Reflect: My heart is blessed. The pure love and life of God pulsate through it in perfect rhythm and order. It is cleansed of all misunderstanding, inharmony, impurity, and disease. There is perfect circulation, perfect respiration, and perfect digestion going on in me constantly. My heart is not the source of life, but life is the creator of my heart. Because life is eternal activity my heart acts in perfect unison with the regular, even, firm, powerful action of life. I do not see nor fear the possibility of losing life, because I see my whole body as the evidence of life's all-powerful presence. My heart is untroubled and unafraid; it is perfect in God's love. I am free from tension, stress, and strain. My blood pressure is normal, my pulse is steady, my heart is strong and whole and perfect.

Breaking Habits

All habits are acquired, not inherited. You can master and overcome any unwanted habit. It is not enough to try to break the habit because you think you should. You must really want to overcome. Work regularly with these thoughts:

Affirm: I am a strong, decisive, confident child of God. I am not dependent upon a habit for my strength or security. My faith is in God within me.

Reflect: God is my resource, my steady, eternal resource. The spirit in me is the Spirit of God, and God cannot long for anything. There is no longer anything in me that feels incomplete or inferior or insecure. My whole being is satisfied and fulfilled. I know what I want to do and be, and I have the faith to

begin, the courage to keep on, and the understanding to know that what I desire and work
for, I already am. I feel equal to every situa-
tion. I do not need material support or stimu-
lation, for God is my strength. I am happy in
my own right, complete and perfect in my
own being, divine and whole right now.

Tension and Hurry

How can we find the time to do the things
that we want and need to do, and to do them
without feeling rushed, hurried, or tense? We
can prayerfully deny these things as having
any part in our life, and set a new theme of
living in tune with the Infinite.

Affirm: I work without strain, walk without hurry, and live without tension, for I am
in tune with the Infinite.

Reflect: I am now established in the peace
and poise of Spirit. I do the things I need to
do easily, efficiently, and effortlessly. I work
with God and thus I work without strain. I do
not hurry, for I know that there is all eternity
to do all that needs to be done. I am in tune
with the rhythm of the universe. There is but

one life, and that life is God. In God there is no time, no deterioration, no aging. With each passing day, I am not older in a waning length of life, but bolder in an expanding depth of life. I am one with the spirit of eternal youth, and I radiate youthful vigor, joy, and enthusiasm. I am relaxed and free, for I am in tune with the Infinite.

Tranquillity

Many of us live under tension and stress, anger, frustration, and irritation. It is possible to learn to live with a relaxed and confident spirit, to find calmness and tranquillity naturally.

Affirm: I am centered in the dynamic spirit of tranquillity. I am refreshed, renewed, and at peace with life and with the world.

Reflect: I am serene and undisturbed as I think of my life and affairs. I am undisturbed by doubt and fear. A quiet surge of peace and power flows through me. My days are uncrowded because I do not waste energy and time in worrying. Even when active, my mind is tranquil, my heart full of patience and love.

I am free from all sense of being overburdened, unappreciated. I am not irritated by weather, mistakes, or interruptions, for my emotions are attuned to the refreshing, healing, harmonizing spirit of tranquillity.

Love

We often hear it said that the greatest thing in the world is love, and yet we overlook the fact that love is also the most needed factor in personal and international relationships. God is love, and as God's child you are a channel through which the limitless and dynamic energy of love can flow—if you let it.

Affirm: I am a channel for the expression of the infinite love of God.

Reflect: The love in me is God in me. I do not generate love, I simply express it. I do not need to make myself love certain people. I need only to get my self out of the way and let the divine energy of love flow through me, as it is its nature to do. I now let love go forth from me universally in all directions. Everyone is lovely to me, and everything is beautiful and meaningful. All hate and hurts are dissolved, and everything is touched into wholeness. This love is the fulfillment of health, happiness, and prosperity in me. It draws me to and draws to me all that which is good and only that which is good. Love flows forth through me in transcendent loveliness—renewing, vitalizing, bringing joy, harmony, and blessing to everything and everyone it touches—and blessing me with emotional, mental, and physical wholeness.

Injustice, Inharmony

There are times when our "rights" are threatened, and when we feel that what is ours is taken from us. The human side of us might resist and struggle. But we are told: *Do not be overcome by evil, but overcome evil with good.* (Rom. 12:21) The way of overcoming is through "coming over" the thoughts of conflict to a higher level, to the thought of divine order.

Affirm: God's law of adjustment regulates all the affairs of my life and all things are in divine order.

Reflect: No one can take from me that

which is rightfully mine. On the human level of appearances it seems that changes can lead to loss and injustice. But beyond the appearance is a level of experience where God's law of adjustment is always active, turning losses into gains, revealing the truth that even if you intended it for evil, God intends it for good. There is that in God that forever works for good like water seeks its own level. No matter what has happened, the law of adjustment is working, regulating, harmonizing, and healing. Divine order is always established within and beyond the experience of confusion.

About the Author

Eric Butterworth is minister of Unity Center of Practical Christianity in New York City, where he has served for over 20 years. He conducts a program of public lectures, growth workshops, and retreats, and his radio broadcasts are heard in four states.

Ordained in 1948, he played a vital role in the organization of the present Association of Unity Churches. He has served churches in Kansas City, Pittsburgh, and Detroit.

He is a frequent contributor to *Unity* magazine. Besides his many popular Unity cassettes, he has published books with Unity, including *In the Flow of Life* and *Spiritual Economics: the prosperity process*.

Mr. Butterworth was born in Canada and raised in California. As his mother was a Unity minister, he was raised with Unity beliefs. He says, "It seems natural to devote my life to the work of helping other people find the influence of Truth in their lives as I have known it in mine."

His wife, Olga, is an associate at the New York center.